John Sell Cotman

John Sell Cotman, author of Antiquities &c.
H. B. Davis del. 1811

British Museum Prints and Drawings Series

John Sell Cotman

Adele M Holcomb

A Colonnade Book

Published by British Museum Publications Limited

Colonnade Books
are published by British Museum Publications
Ltd and are offered as contributions to the
enjoyment, study and understanding of art,
archaeology and history.

The same publishers also produce the official
publications of the British Museum.

© 1978 Adele M. Holcomb

ISBN 0 7141 8004 1   paper
ISBN 0 7141 8005 X   cased

Published by British Museum Publications Ltd,
6 Bedford Square, London WC1B 3RA

Designed by James Shurmer

Set in Monotype Garamond and
printed in Great Britain by W. S. Cowell Ltd

Cover: Mousehold Heath, watercolour, 1809–10

Frontispiece: Mary (Mrs Dawson) Turner,
etched portrait of John Sell Cotman after a
drawing of 1818 by J. P. Davis.

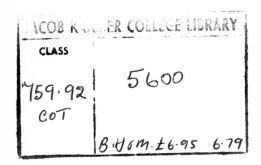

Contents

6 Acknowledgments

7 Introduction

18 Further reading

19 List of British Museum
registration numbers

20 List of Plates

23 Plates

Acknowledgments

The author and publishers are grateful to the following for permission to reproduce pictures:

Plate 36 by gracious permission of H.M. The Queen; 2, Victoria and Albert Museum; 4, Private Collection; 32, Fitzwilliam Museum, Cambridge; 35, Department of Greek and Roman Antiquities, British Museum; 38 Norwich Castle Museum; 41 and 60, Tate Gallery, London.

The remaining plates are from the collection of the Department of Prints and Drawings in the British Museum.

The author and publishers are grateful to F. W. A. Cholmeley, Esq., for permission to quote from the unpublished Cholmeley correspondence deposited in the North Yorkshire Record Office, County Hall, Northallerton.

John Sell Cotman

Distinguished in quality, the British Museum's collection of watercolours, monochrome drawings and prints by John Sell Cotman (1782–1842) displays the full chronological span and in great measure the variety of this gifted Norwich artist's achievement. The collection's character in the main reflects the devotion of James Reeve, curator in the Norwich Museum from 1851 to 1910. Reeve played a major role in laying the basis of Cotman's posthumous reputation and the larger part of his collection of the artist's work was acquired for the nation in 1902. Assembled during a lifetime's study of the Norwich School, the Reeve Cotmans joined Museum holdings that were rich in impressions of Cotman's graphic work and included a number of important early watercolours. A corpus was thus formed in which, apart from oil painting, it is possible to examine all the chief facets of the work of one of the finest and most adventurous artists of the Romantic decades.

John Sell Cotman was born on 16 May 1782 in the northern leet of Coslany in Norwich, the first child of Ann Sell and Edmund Cotman. His father is known to have been a hairdresser in Norwich in 1785, presumably working with his elder brother, John. At some time in his son's later youth, Edmund left barbering; he was listed in the city directory in 1802 as a haberdasher in Cockey Lane (now London Street). John Sell attended Norwich Grammar School where his fondness for drawing was noted, though not cultivated by lessons at the school. Indeed, he appears not to have had any formal training as an artist at any time. The tradition that John Opie, the portrait painter, advised Edmund Cotman in 1798 to let his son 'rather black boots than follow the profession of an artist' suggests that he had very little encouragement in his choice of a calling.

Cotman nevertheless set out to establish himself as an artist in London at the age of sixteen. To support himself he worked as an assistant at Ackermann's Repository of Arts in the Strand before leaving after an unknown interval, 'not being treated as he fancied he ought', according to the later account of his son, Miles Edmund. He was also selling drawings to print dealers and experiencing affronts to his dignity that are depicted fictionally in Jane Porter's *Thaddeus of Warsaw* (1805). Concurrently he produced watercolours that might help establish his reputation. Some of these were shown at Royal Academy exhibitions between 1800 and 1806, while a drawing of a mill (a work that cannot now be securely identified) earned him the Silver Palette of the Society of Arts in 1800.

Just before this success, Cotman had been taken up by Thomas Monro (1759–1833), an amateur who was also Principal Physician to Bethlem Hospital. All but one of Cotman's R.A. exhibitions of 1800 were based on drawings made in the vicinity of Dr Monro's country house in Surrey in 1799. He was probably employed in London by Dr Monro on some form of copying project similar to those on which J. M. W. Turner (1775–1851) and Thomas Girtin (1775–1802) had been engaged by the doctor from *c.*1794 to 1797. It was partly through the relationship with Dr Monro that Cotman's attention was directed to Girtin's style as a model for his early work.

In the novel *Thaddeus of Warsaw*, a print seller who deals fairly with the hard-pressed hero was probably drawn after Peter Norton of Soho Square, whom Cotman later described as his first acquaintance in London. Norton gave the artist an introduction to his brother James in Bristol and in June 1800 Cotman was received by the Bristol Nortons before setting forth on his first extended sketching tour. His itinerary followed a well-trodden path into the Wye Valley, through Brecknockshire to Llandovery and north to Aberystwyth. In Conway he joined a group of artists gathered around the amateur Sir George Beaumont and he may then have had an opportunity to meet Girtin; from Conway his route took him to Caernarvon and Llangollen. Materials garnered on this tour and on a second Welsh trip in 1802 furnished a repertory to which Cotman would turn for motifs throughout his career.

The Museum's *Bridgnorth* (1) dates from his return to England through Shropshire in 1800. Cotman's antic calligraphy stresses the Picturesque character of the bridge with its irregular arches and decrepit toll-house. His graphic style is derived from the highly controlled handwriting of Girtin's watercolours, while a limitation of colour to reddish-brown shades emulates Girtin's tonal restraint (compare *On the Wharfe* 2). In its somewhat hectic alternation of light and dark, *Bridgnorth* is characteristic of Cotman's earliest work.

A flooding movement of light from the middle distance up the surface of a structure immediately above it occurs with greater concentration of effect in the grey monochrome *Cottage in Wales* (3). Against broad washes that evoke the bleakness of mountain scenery, the seemingly half-buried cottage figures as a nearly fantastic presence. The drawing looks ahead to an imaginary subject by Cotman, the *Weird Scene of* 1803 (6). Here a curiously animate quality with which Cotman invested artifacts in the landscape is turned to the interpretation of lines from Ossian: 'We bend towards the voice of the king. The grey-skirted mist is near; the dwelling of the ghosts!' (*Temora*, iii).

Cotman's choice of a theme so alien to the topographical concerns of the watercolour medium was prompted by his membership of the Sketching Society. 'The Brothers', as they initially called themselves, came together in 1799 to organise weekly meetings in which they would draw 'a subject from any Author for the evenings practice which shall be more particularly tending to landscape'. Girtin was the Society's leading talent until his death in 1802. Cotman was not one of the original members; his presence in the Society is first recorded in May 1802 and he continued to be active in it for about four years from that date. The group was concerned to associate with landscape the dignity and significance of history painting, that is, the depiction of traditional figure subjects according to conventions of dramatic legibility and decorum. In the Society, as in many other contexts in British art of the time, the definition of 'history' had become virtually synonymous with the representation of literary themes. The point of the Society's exercises – and it is well exemplified by Cotman's *Weird Scene* – was to make landscape the primary expressive vehicle for ideas suggested by a given text. Its explorations helped mould the attitudes of artists toward landscape and contributed to their new ambitions for the watercolour medium. Cotman's engagement with the Society was highly germane to purposes he conceived for his art in the early years of the nineteenth century.

The example of Turner's success was also immensely stimulating to him. Perhaps the earliest of many Cotman studies after Turner is the Museum's sketch of the Bridgewater Sea-piece (4; compare 5), a popular favourite at the Royal Academy exhibition of 1801. In 1804 the unprecedented monumentality of watercolours exhibited by Turner, *The Passage of the St Gothard* and *Great Fall of the Reichenbach*, had a catalytic influence on the aspirations of watercolourists whose first organisation, the Society of Painters in Water-Colours, was formed in November of the same year. It is likely that the audacity of the *St Gothard*, which measures $40\frac{1}{2} \times 27$ in, inspired Cotman's pencil study of the Via Mala (7).

A large watercolour in which Cotman realised qualities of grandeur akin to Turner's is his *Croyland Abbey* of 1804 (8). At the same time, its feeling for breadth and for delicacy of nuance in the blue tonal scheme belongs to Cotman's sensibility. The massive silhouette of the abbey's west end and its flanking arcades is poised against a majestic sweep of cloud that suggests forces of destruction and repair in the ruin's thousand-year history. With two other 'blue' drawings of similar date in the Museum, *St Mary Redcliffe* and *St Paul's, Morning* (9,12), *Croyland* was owned by the Yarmouth banker and antiquary, Dawson Turner (1775–1859). It was in 1804, when Cotman drew the Museum's portrait of Turner (10), that he first attempted to cultivate Turner's patronage and the latter may have commissioned these drawings.

For *St Mary Redcliffe* Cotman referred to an earlier watercolour of the Bristol church, expanding its scale and authority of design. Blue washes are laid over a brown underpainting, forming a dark range of atmospheric density which fades above and below. From this zone a deft calligraphy gives profiles of gables, chimney-pots, masts, a lime kiln and, in a kind of apotheosis above the tenebrous matrix, St Mary's tower, partly transparent against the dawn. The work's emotional depth is attuned to associations commonly made between the tragedy of Thomas Chatterton (1752–70) and the church near his home where Chatterton's father served as sub-chanter. In Cotman's development, *St Mary Redcliffe* registers a new level of formal mastery and expressive power.

While sketching Croyland in 1804, Cotman had been on his way to visit the Cholmeleys of Brandsby Hall in Yorkshire. His introduction to the family in 1803 came from Teresa Cholmeley's brother, Sir Henry Englefield, whom Cotman probably knew through Dr Monro. Cotman's likeness of Sir Henry (11), presented to his nephew Francis in 1804, augmented a set of family portraits made the previous year. At Brandsby Cotman had been received as a drawing master but was soon regarded by Teresa Cholmeley almost as an adopted son. The Cholmeleys took Cotman to many of the choicest attractions of Yorkshire scenery. While visiting Gormire Lake with Mrs Cholmeley in 1803, Cotman found materials for the Museum's large watercolour of that subject (13). It shows a developed grasp of pictorial structure in its relations of weight and direction within an atmospherically defined space. Rich mottlings and calligraphic accents lend a tactile furnishing to the painted surface, executed mainly in reddish-brown tones.

Gormire was elaborated as an exhibition piece, which was certainly not the case with *Backwater in a Park* (14) of nearly the same date. By comparison its tonal contrasts and textural exuberance appear undisciplined. Still, the elegance of its structure, reminiscent of compositions by Claude Lorrain, seems to rehearse classical tendencies that become salient in Cotman's art of a slightly later time.

Summer visits to Yorkshire in 1803, 1804 and 1805 occasioned many pencil studies of trees. In one of these (15), Cotman isolates the stem and branches, emphasising qualities of relief in the twisting stem and spatial drama in its ramification. A key neatly indicates colours for numbered areas of the drawing. Somewhat later is the tree study (16) in which Cotman focuses not on singularity of shape but on a network of stems, boughs, foliage and space; the touch is much lighter, creating a continuous fabric of line and tone. Integration of solid form and negative space in an overall surface pattern is further pursued in *Larch Trees, Brandsby* (17) which is dated 21 July 1805.

Cotman's studies from nature had their fullest culmination in that year. 'All my Studies have been on the wood above the Bridge', he wrote from Greta Bridge at Rokeby in August, 1805. To Dawson Turner he explained that his summer's work had chiefly been 'colouring from Nature' and many of his studies were 'close copies of that ficle (*sic*) Dame consequently valuable on that account'. Cotman's drawings in colour before the motif mark a new quality of response to sylvan nature, seemingly a world removed from the premeditated tonal invention of *Gormire Lake*. And yet they were no less mediated by considerations of art. The classical balance for example of *Knaresborough Bridge* (18), coloured on the spot, was prepared in the structure of works such as *Gormire* and *Backwater in a Park*, while its fine equivalence of positive form and void was anticipated in the sequence of tree studies.

In its intricacy of foliate mass defined by adjacent recesses of space, *Duncombe Park* (19) conveys the artist's appreciation of luxury of incident in nature. An extraordinarily intimate landscape, it extends the intuition in the later tree studies of nature as a continuously varied surface pattern embracing light, weights and hollows. Subtle variegation of colour in this drawing resembles the muted scheme of greens and greys in *The Drop-Gate, Duncombe Park* (20). For this closed composition, Cotman took a motif of utter inconsequence and made the verticals in the gate – interstices on the right and positive forms on the left – a compelling sequence in which each interval differs subtly from the next.

Most of these studies are associated with Cotman's stay at Rokeby in Yorkshire, where the Cholmeleys had recommended him as a drawing master to Mr and Mrs J. B. S. Morritt. During August 1805 Cotman gave lessons to Mrs Morritt and was shown the beauties of the estate at the junction of the Greta and Tees. 'The scenery of our rivers deserves to become classic ground', J. B. S. Morritt observed in 1811 to Sir Walter Scott. He knew intimately every feature of the surrounding country and was steeped in its ancient associations as the site of a Roman military encampment. Morritt's qualifications as a guide to the Greta woods were further enhanced by his acquaintance with Greek pastoral poetry, from which he published translations in 1802, and it is very likely that his enthusiasms were in some degree conveyed to Cotman. Unpublished correspondence indicates that he ordered a large drawing of the artist's 'Favourite View, from the Mill looking down on the Bridge'; most probably this is the famous watercolour, *Greta Bridge* (25).

Several of the coloured studies of Greta woods favour the closed view that Cotman adopted in *The Drop-Gate*. So it is in *Bank of the Greta* (22) with its airy masses of leafage and cloisonné effect where grey washes define the spaces between slender birch stems. The '*Scotsman's Stone' on the Greta* (23) modifies the incidental tendency of the close focus in its monumental treatment of the boulder. Yet the closed frame is honoured by Cotman's feeling for the immediate surface character of the design; the stone's upward slant to the right responds to the diagonal direction of the current and colour continuities inter-link its form with ranges of greenery above.

Rokeby on the Greta (21) offers a vivid proximity of the pictorial fabric within a brilliantly conceived formal arrangement. Foliage moves in stately cascades down the cliff towards the angle of the foreground bank where geometric shapes of cattle punctuate the junction. From the felicities of this design it is not a far step to the sepia *Pastoral Scene* (26) which extends Cotman's experience of the Greta woods into the imagined realm of a gracious Arcadia.

Cotman's critics have tended to treat the naturalistic impulse of his coloured studies as antithetical to his genius for design. But the intensity of his response to nature in the years around 1805 quickened and informed a classical sensibility; these resources of his style are sympathetically connected. A dialogue between nature and art is indeed the *subject* of much of his work, rather than a reflection of contradictory motives. It is a dialogue in which a sense of the openness of natural process finds form in the discipline of the classical pastoral. Nowhere are these elements more finely adjusted than in the watercolour, *Greta Bridge* (25). Elaborated in a chalk drawing (24), the view looks south towards the single-arch Palladian bridge that is centred in the middle distance, an epitome of Art or of order in its highest sense. The formal purity of the silhouette, weighted by the block of Morritt's Inn on the left, and the geometry of the bridge's reflection, are counterposed against the randomness of nature's patterns in the river banks and boulders.

In September 1805 Cotman reluctantly acceded to Teresa Cholmeley's urging that he 'storm Durham': 'Am I to place it on my studies of trees like a Rookery?' he asked. In his large watercolour (27) the cathedral indeed rests on a pedestal of massed foliage, its complication of Gothic form subsumed in a harmony of coloured planes. Cotman's feeling for atmospheric refinement – frequently denied because it was not expressed in the 'broken tints' used by Turner – is illustrated here in the darkening by cloud shadows of the towers' upper surfaces. Also from the Durham excursion is the chalk drawing, *Castle Eden Dean* (28), akin in its poise and lyricism to *Rokeby on the Greta*.

On his return south Cotman made his last visit to Brandsby. During a two months' stay he gave drawing lessons at Castle Howard and found motifs in which garden ornaments of classical design complement the fluent plenitude of banks of trees. In *Sarcophagus in a Park* (29) the monument is set within a shadowed recess, a shrine-like space centred in a structure of layered planes. Its relief recalls the antique subject of the Oath of the Horatii.

Back in London, Cotman made the final bid of his early career for recognition in the metropolis. He showed several works at the Royal Academy in May 1806 including a drawing, *Horses Drinking*, to which the Museum's sepia of that title (30) is related. But, as revealed in correspondence with the Cholmeleys, he suffered a painful reverse in being rejected for membership in the Water-Colour Society. The popular exhibitions of the Society would have offered him valuable opportunities to sell his work. Following further disappointment in hopes for patronage from the Marquess and Marchioness of Stafford, to whom he gave lessons in the summer of 1806, Cotman made the decision to leave London and open a drawing school in Norwich.

Claiming a new speciality, he advertised himself as a portrait painter at the 1807 exhibition of the newly founded Norwich Society of Artists. Little survives of Cotman's efforts in this vein, but the *Head of a Man in Van Dyck Dress* (31) may be associated with it. In Norwich he was very much in competition with the town's leading drawing master, John Crome (1768–1821). Mary (Mrs Dawson) Turner had for example been taught by Crome for some time when Cotman began to court the Turners' support in 1804. This rivalry may be reflected in the magnificent watercolour of 1804–5, *Dolgelly* (32). Based on the scheme of a much slighter drawing by Crome, Cotman perhaps intended to outdo the older artist in his synthetic breadth of space and in the inventiveness of his patterned surface.

Limited success with the drawing academy prompted Cotman to take new measures. Following his marriage to Ann Miles of Felbrigg in 1809, he announced a circulating collection of six hundred drawings to which subscriptions were solicited. The offer of drawings for copying reflects prevailing practices in the instruction of amateurs in the period. Cotman's repertory was subsequently much expanded but an example that is probably from the original corpus is *Mountain Pass in the Tyrol* (33).

In 1806 Cotman had informed Dawson Turner of his intention to take up oil painting. The ambition to create 'subject' pictures in the new medium is announced by several designs of about this time. In *Centaur Fighting a Lapith* (34) he places a motif derived from the Parthenon metopes, which Cotman may have seen at Lord Elgin's exhibition of the marbles in 1807, in a solemn and graceful landscape that is indebted to the style of the 17th century master Gaspard Dughet (compare the Parthenon metope XXXI, 35 and 36). *The Deluge* (37), also a grey monochrome with a similarly sculptural definition of the figures, was probably based on a late eighteenth-century engraving of a *Deluge* then attributed to Nicolas Poussin. A complex and impressive design datable to *c*.1809, of which an oil painting survives, is *The Judgment of Midas* (38); the Museum's drawing of this subject was made in connection with Cotman's later experiments with soft-ground etching, in 1814 (39,75). In its subject from Ovid's *Metamorphoses*, Midas overhears the musical contest of Pan and Apollo and prefers Pan's rustic melodies; for arguing against the verdict of Timolus he will be given asses' ears. The work is an allegory of Nature, personified by the Arcadian god who performs in a bower of vegetation, and the Apollonian realm of Art represented by tectonic forms towards which the figures of a centaur and a youth gesture.

In *Breaking the Clod* (40), screens of foliage frame lattice-like openings where stems are inscribed against the light. The finesse of the drawing's arrangement and its suggestion of bucolic harmony seem an extension of the landscape scheme of an early oil, *Duncombe Park* (41). While probably not Cotman's, the title of the drawing from Virgil's *Georgics* ('Much service does he do the land who with the mattock breaks up the sluggish clods') is in the spirit of his motif.

The pastoral mode that Cotman developed around 1805 was thus carried forward during his Norwich years, and beyond. But he worked concurrently in several veins of subject matter. Sea-painting had attracted him early on and in *The Dismasted Brig* (42) he created an almost lapidary image of a distressed ship fixed at the hub of turbulent forces. Its potency of symbolic allusion is matched by Cotman's formal power in suggesting reflective surface and transparent depth with arresting economy. *Yarmouth River* (43) is built around the rhythmic convergence of cloud masses at the crosspiece of a mast; it is a fine example of the broad, dry handling Cotman adopted in some watercolours of *c*.1809 where we find pebbled textures within the washes.

Many of Cotman's watercolours from the years 1807 to 1811 emphasise Picturesque idiosyncrasy in portraying subjects with a strongly local character. *Fisherman's Cottage, Thorpe* (44) is rich in such features as the irregular intervals of a ladder against the cottage door. A kindred subject is that of the *Yarmouth Fishwoman* (45), a well-known local character whose oddity of presence is established by the disengagement with which Cotman has organised the coloured areas of the design. *Powis Castle* (46), with its textural vagaries, and the *Bridge at Saltram, South Devon* (47) participate in the same tendency of the artist at this period to dwell on what is erratic and characterful in local scenery. It is as though Cotman's attention to the fortuity of nature in his Greta subjects has shifted to a new aspect of visual accident, one which is perhaps more plebeian, certainly more local in his manifestations. The large *Mousehold Heath* (48) is a supreme instance of this grasp of locality with its splaying of paths that make a salient network against the slopes, yet also serve to plot their shifts of contour.

The Screen, Norwich Cathedral (49) is one of several drawings of the interior of the cathedral that Cotman executed around 1807, probably with the encouragement of Dawson Turner (who owned the watercolour of Durham). Delicacy of definition in the screen is extended in the fine reticulations of borders between coloured washes, chiefly warm yet reticent harmonies of yellow and grey. The passageway to the ambulatory on the right and the door open on stairs to a gallery belong to a poetry of entrances that Cotman favoured in many of his architectural subjects.

Through the urging of Dawson Turner and the hope of tapping a new clientele, Cotman became increasingly active as an etcher of antiquities from 1810 on. His first prints, the *Miscellaneous Etchings* (1811) dedicated to Sir Henry Englefield (50), prominently include such subjects as the 'Saxo-Norman Doorway' of Kirkham Priory and the ruins of North Creake Abbey. 'I decidedly *follow* Piranesi', Cotman wrote in 1811 with regard to his graphic work, which is however attuned to Picturesque incident rather than to Baroque tonal opulence. Depicting the remains of a twelfth-century Cistercian Abbey, *The Old College House, Conway* (51) draws on Cotman's Welsh cottage imagery in its low viewpoint and steep diagonal recession, its textural corrugations and scattered spaces among the oriel panes. In *Trees in Duncombe Park, Yorkshire* (52,53) he tried to maintain his own bent as an artist; as in the watercolour of this name, the fabric of parkland surrounding a shadowed recess suggests an analogy to the contemplating mind. The daughters of Teresa Cholmeley, now deceased, praised the 'trees at Duncombe Park . . . as most like Rembrandts', but their brother Francis reported that the view was not generally approved, 'because it might have been *anywhere*'.

Opinions of the latter kind supported Cotman's entirely antiquarian scope in *The Architectural Antiquities of Norfolk*, begun in July 1811 and completed in 1818. Outstanding among these sixty etched views is that of the South Gate at Yarmouth (54), a relic of the town's fourteenth-century enclosure. The imposing mass of the towers in Cotman's print presides with a certain domestic hubris over a range of humble structures and casual activity. This first plate of the series was dedicated to Dawson Turner. Another, which depicts with great élan St Benet's Abbey (55), also a subject joining medieval remains with the apparatus of useful work, is inscribed to Cotman's chief pupil, Mrs Turner.

Cotman had in fact moved with his family to Yarmouth in 1812 at her husband's instance and was largely occupied there in instructing Mary Turner and the elders of the family's six daughters. He thus superseded Crome as the household's principal drawing master. His remaining time for the next decade was devoted almost exclusively to antiquarian publications promoted by Dawson Turner. An occasional etching such as *Grand Bonfire at the Yarmouth Festival* (56) and the drawing after his *Judgment of Midas* (both of 1814) are among the few works of this time that are unconnected with architectural etching. Cotman's decision in 1812 to make himself so dependent upon one source of patronage was not reached without severe mental conflict and an ensuing period of physical illness.

Chief among the undertakings to which Turner urged him was the *Architectural Antiquities of Normandy*. Cotman invested high hopes in this project for the securing of his reputation and in its preparation made trips to Normandy in 1816, 1817 and 1820. He worked in pencil on these journeys; sepia washes were added later to his characterisation of form in such studies as *Arches of the Cloister of St Georges de Boscherville* (58) of 1818. Before his first tour Cotman had been given a camera lucida by Sir Henry Englefield and in 1817 employed this projecting device to make drawings for his ambitious etching of the west front of Rouen Cathedral (59). Concern for accuracy of detail and the twenty or so weeks' labour of achieving it virtually precluded pictorial effect in this etching. But many of the Normandy plates transcend their documentary purpose. *The Crypt of the Trinity at Caen* (62) is notable for its sombre monumentality and for the subtlety of its management of light and dark. Castle subjects like the *Château Gaillard* (60,61) and the *Castle at Dieppe* (63) combine a panoramic amplitude with the solidity of structure found in Cotman's best work.

During the artist's 1820 tour he declared his intention to follow the *Architectural Antiquities* with a book of etchings on Picturesque Normandy. The announcement came immediately after an account of his exhilaration between Domfront and Mortain, on an 'artist's day, [with] fine clouds, the shadows of which gave life & spirit to everything . . . '. A group of sepia drawings prepared for this uncompleted project is represented by the *Town of Mortain with Mont St Michel* (64). In this unfinished drawing, starkly crystalline rock forms frame the undulations of wooded hills. The Norman fortress that figures in the far distance held a compelling fascination for Cotman; he made it the subject of a design in several watercolour versions, for example the Museum's resplendent *Mont St Michel* (65).

The Architectural Antiquities of Normandy appeared in 1822 with letterpress by Dawson Turner. Response to the work fell far short of the acclaim for which Cotman had hoped and he underwent a severe depression that lasted from June 1822 into the next year. In December 1823 he returned with his family to Norwich to set up again as a drawing master; the field there was more open since Crome's death in 1821. Normandy subjects helped furnish an expanded collection of drawing copies, as in the *View on the River Sarthe near Alençon* (66). Cotman's exhibition drawings following his move back to Norwich show a heightened intensity of colour that reflects broad tendencies in English watercolour of the 1820s. With richness of hue he adopted frequently a Picturesque *rocaille* of architectural detail drawn with the brush; watercolours of this kind, illustrated by *Old Houses in Normandy* (67), appealed to a taste that had been initiated by the Continental scenes of Samuel Prout (1783–1852).

Stimulated anew, Cotman's aspirations as an artist flourished in various directions in this decade. Once more he became active as an oil painter. The splendid drawing of

Norwich Castle (68) of 1825, its Poussinesque gravity tempered by lyrical qualities of movement and atmosphere, is a study for a picture in oils. Similar in its lushness of effect to Cotman's oils of the 1820s is the treatment of light in the watercolour called *Château in Normandy* (69) though its motif seems to be a variant of a Yorkshire subject.

Luminosity was very much an object in Cotman's attention to J. M. W. Turner's work at this time. His *Norham Castle on the Tweed* (71) is one of several studies of mezzotints after Turner designs (70) in W. B. Cooke's *Rivers of England* (1823–1827) and the series may well have influenced the itinerary of Cotman's Thames and Medway tour of 1828 (78, 79). His drawings after Turner's *Liber Studiorum* probably date from the early 1830s, judging from Cotman's statement in 1834 that he had hoped for over two years to publish a work in mezzotint similar to Turner's *Liber*. What he admired in this model is illustrated by his study after *The Junction of the Severn and Wye* (compare 72 and 73) in its suffused light and tonal resonance. It is also characteristic of Cotman's preference for the Claudian scenes among Turner's categories of landscape. Oddly enough, the book published as Cotman's *Liber Studiorum* (74–77) in 1838 was not the intended work in mezzotint. It was named by H. G. Bohn, purchaser and publisher under this title of the plates of soft-ground etchings that Cotman had made between 1810 and *c*.1815, prints that had not been conceived as a corpus or as related to Turner's epitome of his landscape art.

Cotman's exploration of the soft-ground medium was probably recommended by its popularity in the illustration of drawing manuals, as in publications by Louis Francia and Samuel Prout, during the second decade of the nineteenth century. Direct reproduction of the texture of pencil drawings by soft-ground etching was considered an aid in the instruction of amateurs. Ever in the rear of developments in his plans for commercial success, Cotman indicated a forthcoming work on landscape composition (never realised) which would almost certainly have been a drawing manual when he exhibited his soft-ground etchings at the Norwich Society in 1824. By this date lithography had largely superseded the soft-ground medium and drawing as an amateur pastime was declining.

During the later 1820s Cotman trained his eldest son Miles Edmund (1810–53) as his assistant and, between recurring attacks of depression, tried to attract patronage for his work. By the early 1830s he had mainly abandoned oil painting. Experiment with a thickening agent in watercolour, thought to have been derived from rotting flour paste, yielded the medium of such drawings as *Bamborough Castle* (81). In this design Cotman realised a choreography of motion that reaches from a declivity at the right to the plateau left of centre, accented climactically by spots of colour, and then concluded in a sweep of light. Breadth and complication of pictorial movement in continuities of line and tonal mass are salient features of Cotman's work in the 1830s. A splendid instance is *Postwick Grove* (82), also executed in the opaque medium, where the main rhythmic sequence moves towards, around and away from a shadowed centre, touched with red in the figure. Textural values are conspicuous in many of these 'paste' drawings. The forceful and spare *Cader Idris* (83) suggests through the apparent physical manipulation of the paint the sculptural contours of its subject.

In 1834 Cotman was reprieved from a deteriorating situation as drawing master in Norwich by his appointment as Professor of Drawing at King's College, London. Intensely elated at first by this change of fortune, he was brought down for a time when persuaded by family pressure and Dawson Turner to sell his extensive collections of books, prints and casts. The auction was indicated as a means of paying debts and the costs of removal from Norwich, but the prices realised for Cotman's own paintings sadly revealed a lack of local esteem for his work. Established finally with his family in London, Cotman was settled there for the remainder of his life.

At the College he taught with the aid of a greatly enlarged collection of drawing copies, many of them produced by Miles Edmund, his sister Ann (b.1812) and youngest brother Alfred Henry (b.1819), all in the style of Cotman *père*. Despite improved material security, Cotman's production as an artist was intermittent; it nevertheless includes some supremely beautiful drawings. The firmness of structure and rhythmic grace of *Benthe Tor* (84) and of *Mountains and Lake, North Wales* (85) are representative of the quality of Cotman's landscape compositions on coloured paper in this period. *Heidelberg Castle* (86), a pencil design that was replicated in watercolour, recalls the handling of Cotman's studies after Turner's *Liber*, with a more ample and complex play of tonal gesture. His continued admiration for Turner's *Liber* is indeed attested by the chalk drawing *Cephalus and Procris* (87), an invention in the pastoral ambiance of Turner's print of the same subject. For his *Boys Fishing* (88), a chalk and watercolour drawing associated with an oil probably dating from 1839, Cotman looked back to the eighteenth-century pastorals of Gainsborough; the intensity of raking light is expressed in a harlequin pattern of colour and shade in the figures, its brilliance set against tonal luxuriance and cursive rhythms in the foliage.

Not long after the presumed date of *Boys Fishing*, Cotman was disabled by a depression that persisted into 1841. Recovery at last was marked by the return of his collector's zeal – gleefully he reported buying for £10 a Jordaens copy of Rubens's *Judgment of Paris* – and the desire to visit Norfolk again. Many of the finest drawings dating from Cotman's eight-week holiday in the autumn of 1841 are in the Museum's collection. Travelling by steamer from Norwich to Yarmouth on October 2, he drew *River Bank with Trees* (89), expecting that he might work it up as a picture to judge from such notations as 'Pure Sky Excepting Glow (—?) Clouds of Cream' in the upper left. The motif in this sketch of a frieze of trees suspended in the middle distance reappears in *The Wold Afloat* (90). Both this drawing and *Below Langley* (91) are dated 19 October when storms flooded the countryside around Norwich. It is tempting to find portents in Cotman's response to the lifting of winds that sweep across this scene, the rising flight of birds, the windmills braced against the gale.

Sky Effect near Yarmouth (92) and *Storm off Cromer* (93) offer stark confrontations with space. In the latter, an ellipse of shoreline is echoed in the rounded profile of the upper border, enclosing an expanse that is qualified only by the line of the horizon. Its play between a suggested depth of space and undifferentiated surface pattern seems to anticipate compositions by Courbet and Whistler in the 1850s and 60s. Two drawings of the Yarmouth Road, two of Blofield and *The Pound at Blickling* (94–98) return to the amenities of Cotman's domestic pastoral. Executed in black and white chalk on grey paper, the last of these is one of the most festive of the Norfolk designs, with its effervescence of leafage and a niche within the woods where mullion-like stems are picked out in white. Delicacy and grace of movement characterise others like the *Old Yarmouth Road from Norwich* (94) in which tree forms and their shadows perform a kind of minuet across the path.

Intended for translation into oil, *Mousehold Heath* (100) opposes a weighting of hollows to the broad convexity of the horizon. Only one painting based on the Norfolk drawings survives, an oil in the Norwich Castle Museum deriving from two British Museum designs called *From my Father's House at Thorpe* (101,102). The drawings transform a modest location on the Yare into an elegant parkland that descends in a flowing but dignified cadence towards the light-filled river. Gestural grace, the prodigality of natural form and the balance of tectonic order – these touchstones of Cotman's art are marvellously embodied in the Thorpe designs.

Cotman lapsed into depression before completing the painting. By June 1842 he was gravely ill, though the doctors found no specific malady or serious danger. On 24 July he expired, his death attributed to 'Natural Decay'.

'Among the most perfect water-colours ever made', Laurence Binyon wrote in 1939 of Cotman's *Greta Bridge*. 'Perfection' surely addresses the artist's refinement of means, a profound quality of finesse that is rare in the traditions of Western art. But Cotman's formal authority is intimately associated in his work of about 1805 with a vision of nature steeped in the mood of ancient bucolic poetry. He figures as one of the most gifted and inventive participants in the development of the pastoral mode in Romantic landscape. His later work extended the structural probity of the Greta drawings, contributing to a European as well as English tendency to invest landscape with the discipline of neo-classical sensibility. Through his *Architectural Antiquities of Normandy* Cotman indeed had an acknowledged impact on French art, particularly on painters like the young Corot who have been called the 'statuaries' of landscape. Cotman's sensitivity to pictorial structure was enriched by a radical questioning of the nature of the artist's means, of the independent virtualities of the elements of picture-making. His exploratory openness was matched in early nineteenth-century art only by the experimentalism of Turner.

Further reading

Hardie, Martin, 'Cotman's Water-colours: The Technical Aspect,' *Burlington Magazine*, July 1942.

Hawcroft, Francis W., 'Three Works by Cotman,' *Burlington Magazine*, February 1962.

Holcomb, Adele M., '*Devil's Den*: An Early Drawing by John Sell Cotman,' *Master Drawings*, Winter 1973.

Kay, H. Isherwood, ed., 'John Sell Cotman's Letters from Normandy, 1817–1820,' Walpole Society annual volumes xiv and xv (1926 and 1927).

Kitson, Sydney, *The Life of John Sell Cotman*, London, 1937.

Oppé, A. P., 'Cotman and his Public,' *Burlington Magazine*, July 1942.

Oppé, A. P., *The Water-colour Drawings of John Sell Cotman*, Special Number, *The Studio*, 1923.

Rajnai, Miklos, assisted by Marjorie Allthorpe-Guyton, *John Sell Cotman: Drawings of Normandy in Norwich Castle Museum*, Norwich, 1975.

List of British Museum registration numbers

Frontispiece	1859.5.22.8	59	1859.5.28.6
1	1902.5.14.8	61	1859.5.28.8
3	1902.5.14.38	62	1859.5.28.5
5	1902.5.14.284	63	1859.5.28.6
6	1902.5.14.39	64	1902.5.14.56
7	1902.5.14.135*	65	1958.7.12.330
8	1859.5.28.118	66	1902.5.14.120
9	1859.5.28.117	67	1948.4.10.9
10	1902.5.14.215	68	1902.5.14.123
11	1902.5.14.72	69	1902.5.14.36
12	1859.2.28.122	70	R.756
13	1958.7.12.329	71	1902.5.14.283
14	1902.5.14.7	72	R.28
15	1902.5.14.294	73	1902.5.14.268
16	1902.5.14.309	74	1902.5.14.1154
17	1902.5.14.293	75	1878.10.12.472
18	1902.5.14.9	76	1902.5.14.115
19	1902.5.14.13	77	1902.5.14.595
20	1902.5.14.14	78	1902.5.14.136
21	1902.5.14.110	79	1902.5.14.126
22	1902.5.14.10	80	1902.5.14.127
23	1902.5.14.12	81	1902.5.14.30
24	1902.5.14.76	82	1902.5.14.29
25	1902.5.14.17	83	1902.5.14.26
26	1885.5.9.1400	84	1902.5.14.98
27	1859.5.28.119	85	1902.5.14.102
28	1902.5.14.43	86	1902.5.14.91
29	1859.5.28.121	87	1902.5.14.137
30	1902.5.14.41*	88	1902.5.15.58
31	1902.5.14.15	89	1902.5.14.142
33	1902.5.14.16	90	1902.5.14.146
34	1902.5.14.41	91	1902.5.14.145
37	1902.5.14.40	92	1902.5.14.140
39	1902.5.14.111	93	1902.5.14.160
40	1902.5.14.44	94	1902.5.14.118
42	1902.5.14.32	95	1902.5.14.167
43	1859.5.28.116	96	1902.5.14.116
44	1902.5.14.25	97	1902.5.14.105
45	1902.5.14.22	98	1902.5.14.156
46	1902.5.14.24	99	1902.5.14.158
47	1902.5.14.21	100	1902.5.14.164
48	1902.5.14.20	101	1902.5.14.165
49	1902.5.14.18	102	1902.5.14.166
50	1871.8.12.2916		
51	1865.5.20.474		
52	1902.5.14.256		
53	1902.5.14.257		
54	1859.5.28.2		
55	1858.5.28.2		
56	1902.5.14.1118		
57	1902.5.14.179		
58	1902.5.14.53		

List of Plates

Except as otherwise specified, all works by Cotman.

Frontispiece Mary (Mrs Dawson) Turner, etched portrait of John Sell Cotman after a drawing of 1818 by J. P. Davis.

1 *Bridgnorth*, watercolour, d.1800.

2 Thomas Girtin, *On the Wharfe*, watercolour, Victoria & Albert Museum, 1798.

3 *Cottage in Wales*, monochrome watercolour, *c.*1800.

4 J. M. W. Turner, *Bridgewater Sea-piece*, exhibited 1801.

5 Study after Turner's *Bridgewater Sea-piece*, pencil, probably 1801.

6 *Weird Scene*, monochrome watercolour, d. 23 March 1803.

7 *Via Mala*, pencil, probably 1804.

8 *Croyland Abbey*, watercolour, 1803–4.

9 *St Mary Redcliffe*, watercolour, *c.*1803.

10 Portrait of Dawson Turner, pencil, d. 2 August 1804.

11 Portrait of Sir Henry Englefield, pencil, inscribed to Francis Cholmeley and d. 5 July 1804.

12 *St Paul's, Morning*, watercolour, *c.*1803.

13 *Gormire Lake, Yorkshire*, watercolour, 1803–4.

14 *Backwater in a Park*, watercolour, *c.*1803.

15 *Tree Study* (–294), pencil, 1803–4.

16 *Tree Study* (–309), pencil, 1803–4.

17 *Larch Trees, Brandsby*, pencil, d. 21 July 1805.

18 *Bridge at Knaresborough*, watercolour, 1805.

19 *Duncombe Park*, watercolour, 1805.

20 *The Drop-Gate, Duncombe Park*, watercolour, 1805.

21 *Rokeby on the Greta*, pencil with red chalk, 1805.

22 *Bank of the Greta*, watercolour, 1805.

23 *The 'Scotsman's Stone' on the Greta*, watercolour, 1805.

24 Study for *Greta Bridge*, chalk, 1805.

25 *Greta Bridge*, watercolour, 1805.

26 *Pastoral Scene*, sepia, *c.*1806.

27 *Durham Cathedral*, watercolour, 1805.

28 *Castle Eden Dean*, chalk on bluish-grey paper with touches of wash, 1805.

29 *Sarcophagus in a Park*, watercolour, *c.*1806.

30 *Horses Drinking*, sepia, 1806.

31 *Head of a Man in Van Dyck Dress*, watercolour, probably 1807.

32 *Dolgelly*, watercolour, Fitzwilliam Museum, Cambridge, 1804–5.

33 *Mountain Pass in the Tyrol*, watercolour, probably 1809.

34 *Centaur Fighting a Lapith*, monochrome, probably 1807.

35 *Centaur and Lapith*, metope XXXI from the Parthenon, British Museum, *c.*447–443 BC.

36 Gaspard Dughet (1613–75), *A Landscape with a Waterfall*, oil on canvas, coll. H.M. the Queen.

37 *The Deluge*, monochrome, probably 1807.

38 *The Judgment of Midas*, oil on canvas, Castle Museum, Norwich, *c*.1809.

39 *The Judgment of Midas*, pencil, d. 1814.

40 *Breaking the Clod*, chalk with wash on brownish paper touched with white, *c*.1807.

41 *Duncombe Park*, oil on canvas, Tate Gallery, 1806–7.

42 *The Dismasted Brig*, watercolour, *c*.1807.

43 *Yarmouth River*, watercolour, *c*.1809–10.

44 *Fisherman's Cottage, Thorpe*, watercolour, *c*.1810.

45 *Yarmouth Fishwoman*, watercolour, *c*.1812.

46 *Powis Castle*, watercolour, *c*.1810.

47 *Bridge at Saltram, South Devon*, watercolour, *c*.1810.

48 *Mousehold Heath*, watercolour, 1809–10.

49 *The Screen, Norwich Cathedral*, watercolour, *c*.1807.

50 Dedication to Sir Henry Englefield, *Miscellaneous Etchings*, 1811.

51 *The Old College House, Conway, North Wales, Miscellaneous Etchings*, 1811.

52 *Trees in Duncombe Park, Yorkshire*, pencil study for etching.

53 *Trees in Duncombe Park, Yorkshire, Miscellaneous Etchings*, 1811.

54 *South Gate, Yarmouth*, etching, *The Architectural Antiquities of Norfolk*, 1811–18.

55 *St Benet's Abbey*, etching, *The Architectural Antiquities of Norfolk*, 1811–18.

56 *Grand Bonfire at the Yarmouth Festival*, soft ground etching with colour, d. 19 April 1814.

57 *A Street in Yarmouth*, pencil, *c*.1815.

58 *Arches of the Cloister of St Georges de Boscherville*, pencil and sepia, d. 3 July 1818, 1821 (possibly because sepia was added at later date).

59 *West Front of Rouen Cathedral*, etching, *The Architectural Antiquities of Normandy*, 1822.

60 *Château Gaillard*, monochrome drawing in preparation for etching, Tate Gallery, insc. 'Sketched July 24, 1818'.

61 *Château Gaillard*, etching, *The Architectural Antiquities of Normandy*, 1822.

62 *Crypt of the Abbey Church of the Holy Trinity at Caen*, etching, *The Architectural Antiquities of Normandy*, 1822.

63 *Castle at Dieppe*, etching, *The Architectural Antiquities of Normandy*, 1822.

64 *The Town of Mortain with Mont St Michel*, sepia, 1820–23.

65 *Mont St Michel*, watercolour, *c*.1825.

66 *View on the River Sarthe near Alençon*, pencil, d. 24 December, 1823.

67 *Old Houses in Normandy*, watercolour, 1823–28.

68 Study for a painting of Norwich Castle, black and white chalk on bluish-grey paper, d. 5 April 1825.

69 *Château in Normandy*, watercolour, *c*.1828.

70 J. M. W. Turner, *Norham Castle on the Tweed*, mezzotint, *The Rivers of England*, 1823–27.

71 Drawing after Turner's *Norham Castle on the Tweed*, pencil, 1824–28.

72 J. M. W. Turner, *The Junction of the Severn and Wye*, mezzotint, 1811, *Liber Studiorum*.

73 Study after Turner's *Junction of the Severn and Wye*, pencil, *c*.1832.

74 *Tan y Beolch*, soft ground etching (design dates from *c*.1806). Cotman's *Liber Studiorum*, published 1838.

75 *Judgment of Midas*, soft ground etching (design dates from *c*.1809). Cotman's *Liber Studiorum*, published 1838.

76 *Postwick Grove*, black chalk heightened with white, *c*.1814. Cotman's *Liber Studiorum*, published 1838.

77 *Postwick Grove*, soft ground etching. Cotman's *Liber Studiorum*, published 1838.

78 *Hayboat on the Medway*, pencil, probably 1828.

79 *Dreadnought on the Thames*, pencil, d. 8 January 1828.

80 *Fire at Vinegar Works on the Yare*, pencil with coloured chalk and touches of body colour, 1829.

81 *Bamborough Castle*, watercolour, *c*.1830.

82 *Postwick Grove* (–29), watercolour, *c*.1835.

83 *Cader Idris*, watercolour, *c*.1835.

84 *Benthe Tor*, pencil heightened with white on blue paper, *c*.1836.

85 *Mountains and Lake, North Wales*, pencil heightened with white on brown paper, *c*.1839.

86 *Heidelberg Castle*, pencil, *c*.1834.

87 *Cephalus and Procris*, black and white chalk on brown paper, *c*.1839.

88 *Landscape with Boys Fishing*, brush and ink with body colour on blue paper, probably 1839.

89 *River Bank with Trees*, black and white chalk on brown paper, d. 2 October 1841.

90 *The Wold Afloat*, black and white chalk on grey paper, d. 19 October 1841.

91 *Below Langley*, black chalk heightened with white on grey-brown paper, d. 19 October 1841.

92 *Sky Effect near Yarmouth*, black chalk heightened with white on blue paper, 1841.

93 *Storm off Cromer*, black and white chalk on brown paper, d. 14 November 1841.

94 *Blofield: The Old Yarmouth Road from Norwich*, black and white chalk on brown paper, 1841.

95 *Blofield: The Old Yarmouth Road to Norwich*, black and white chalk on grey-brown paper, d. November 1841.

96 *Hollow Way at Blofield*, black chalk heightened with white on blue paper, 1841.

97 *At Blofield near Norwich, Deer in a Glade*, pencil, chalk and body colour on brown paper, 1841.

98 *The Pound at Blickling*, black and white chalk on grey paper, d. 10 November 1841.

99 *Landscape with Rainbow*, black and white chalk on brown paper, d. 18 November, 1841.

100 *Mousehold Heath* (–164), black and white chalk on brown paper, 1841.

101 *From my Father's House at Thorpe*, black and white chalk, 1841.

102 *From my Father's House at Thorpe: View with Firs*, black and white chalk on grey-brown paper, 1841.

The Plates

1 *Bridgnorth*, watercolour, d.1800. 16 × 28·3 cm.

2 Thomas Girtin, *On the Wharfe*, watercolour, Victoria & Albert Museum, 1798.

3 *Cottage in Wales*, monochrome watercolour, *c*.1800. 17·3 × 24·8cm.

4 J. M. W. Turner, *Bridgewater Sea-piece*, exhibited 1801.

5 Study after Turner's *Bridgewater Sea-piece*, pencil, probably 1801. 14 × 19·2cm.

6 *Weird Scene*, monochrome watercolour, d. 23 March 1803. 21·2 × 31·4cm.

7 *Via Mala*, pencil, probably 1804. 29·6 × 21·1cm.

8 *Croyland Abbey*, watercolour, 1803–4. 29.9 × 54.4cm.

9 *St Mary Redcliffe*, watercolour, *c.*1803. 37·1 × 53·4cm.

10 Portrait of Dawson Turner, pencil, d. 2 August 1804. 30 × 22·2cm.

11 Portrait of Sir Henry Englefield, pencil, inscribed to Francis Cholmeley and d. 5 July 1804. 17·7 × 15·6cm.

12 *St Paul's, Morning*, watercolour, *c*.1803. 19·6 × 32·2 cm.

13 *Gormire Lake, Yorkshire*, watercolour, 1803–4. 37·2 × 54·7cm.

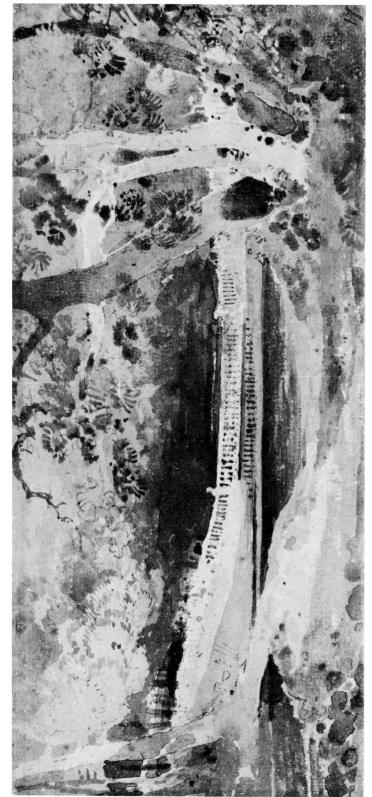

14 *Backwater in a Park*, watercolour, c.1803. 14·4 × 31·4cm.

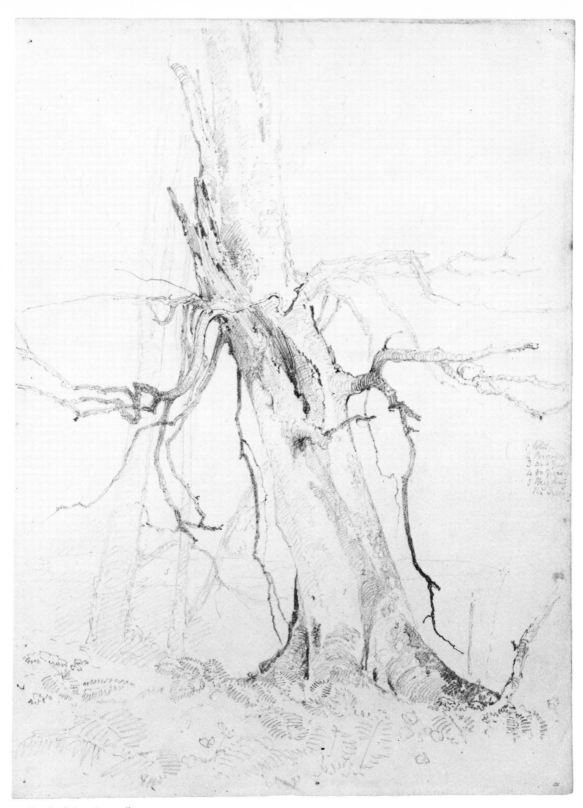

15 *Tree Study* (–294), pencil, 1803–4. 35·2 × 25·9cm.

16 *Tree Study* (–309), pencil, 1803–4. 30·7 × 25·1cm.

17 *Larch Trees, Brandsby*, pencil, d. 21 July 1805. 30·4 × 24·6cm.

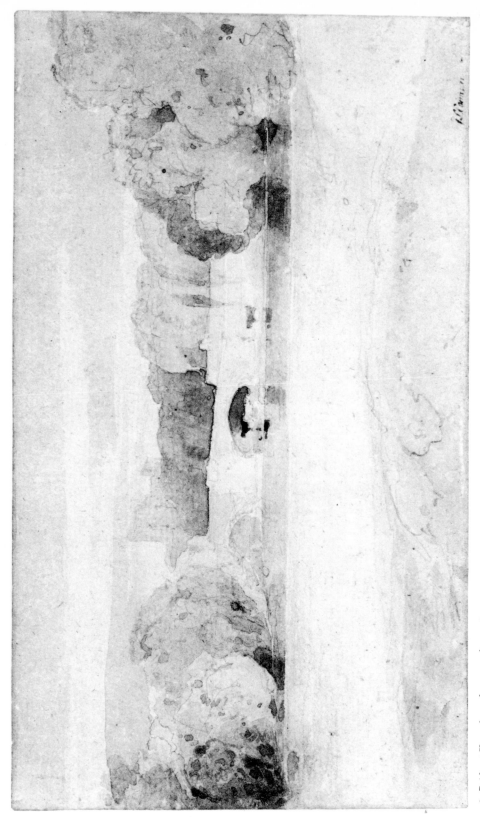

18 *Bridge at Knaresborough*, watercolour, 1805. 13·7 × 23·2cm.

19 *Duncombe Park*, watercolour, 1805. 32·8 × 23cm.

20 *The Drop-Gate, Duncombe Park*, watercolour, 1805. 33 × 23·1cm.

21 *Rokeby on the Greta*, pencil with red chalk, 1805. 20·5 × 13·7 cm.

22 *Bank of the Greta*, watercolour, 1805. 22·4 × 33cm.

46

23 *The 'Scotsman's Stone' on the Greta*, watercolour, 1805. 26·3 × 39·6cm.

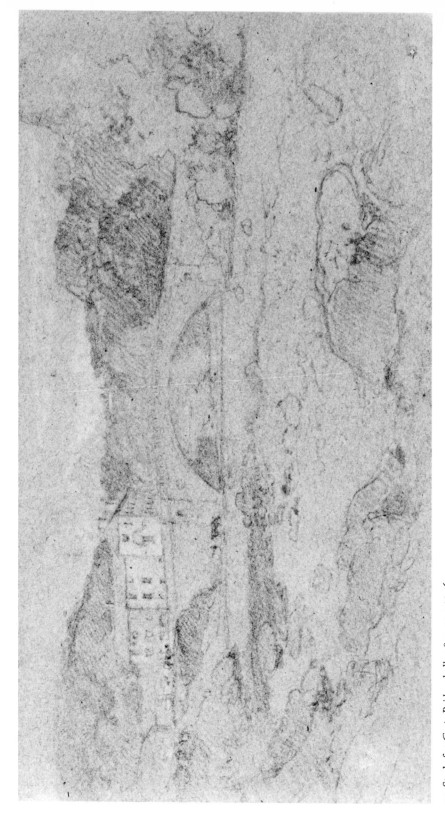

24 Study for *Greta Bridge*, chalk, 1805. 14·1 × 26cm.

25 *Greta Bridge*, watercolour, 1805. 22·7 × 32·9cm.

26 *Pastoral Scene*, sepia, *c.*1806. 31·6 × 21·8cm.

27 *Durham Cathedral*, watercolour, 1805. 43·9 × 33·4cm.

28 *Castle Eden Dean,* chalk on bluish-grey paper with touches of wash, 1805. 20·9 × 23·4cm.

29 *Sarcophagus in a Park*, watercolour, c.1806. 33 × 21·6cm.

30 *Horses Drinking*, sepia, 1806. 27·9 × 20·9cm.

31 *Head of a Man in Van Dyck Dress*, watercolour, probably 1807. 31·2 × 21cm.

32 *Dolgelly*, watercolour, Fitzwilliam Museum, Cambridge, 1804–5.

33 *Mountain Pass in the Tyrol*, watercolour, probably 1809. 22 × 28·5 cm.

34 *Centaur Fighting a Lapith,* monochrome, probably 1807. 32·8 × 22·3cm.

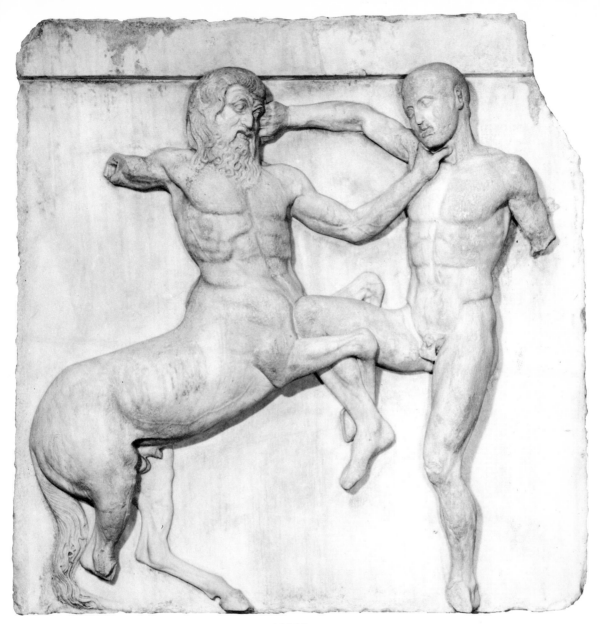

35 *Centaur and Lapith*, metope XXXI from the Parthenon, British Museum, *c*.447–443BC.

36 Gaspard Dughet (1613–75), *A Landscape with a Waterfall*, oil on canvas, coll. H.M. the Queen.

37 *The Deluge*, monochrome, probably 1807. 32·1 × 22·7cm.

38 *The Judgment of Midas,* oil on canvas, Castle Museum, Norwich, *c.*1809.

39 *The Judgment of Midas*, pencil, d.1814. 17·4 × 24·9 cm.

40 *Breaking the Clod,* chalk with wash on brownish paper touched with white, *c.*1807. 31·9 × 26·3cm.

41 *Duncombe Park*, oil on canvas, Tate Gallery, 1806–7.

42 *The Dismasted Brig*, watercolour, *c.*1807. 20 × 30·9cm.

43 *Yarmouth River*, watercolour, c.1809–10. 23·9 × 34cm.

44 *Fisherman's Cottage, Thorpe,* watercolour, *c.*1810. 26·8 × 21·2cm.

45 *Yarmouth Fishwoman*, watercolour, *c.*1812. 23·4 × 16cm.

46 *Powis Castle*, watercolour, c.1810. 19·3 × 25·7cm.

47 *Bridge at Saltram, South Devon*, watercolour, c.1810. 18·8 × 27cm.

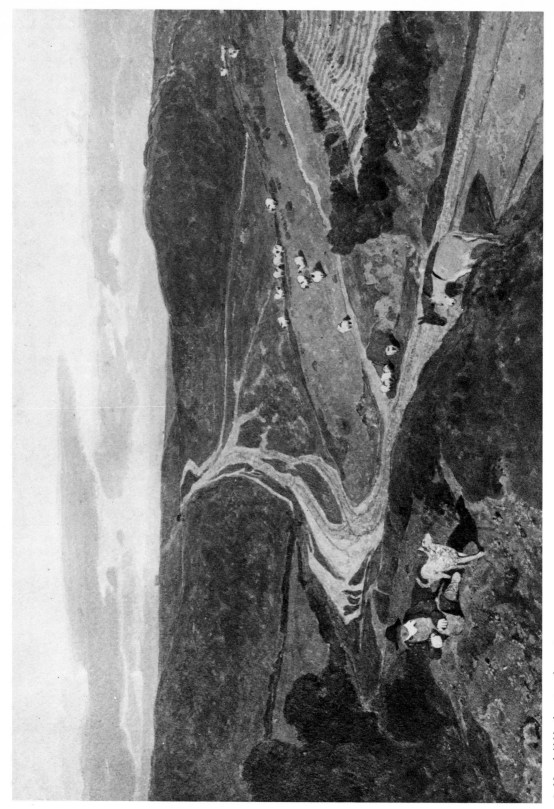

48 *Mousehold Heath*, watercolour, 1809–10, 30 × 43·5cm.

49 *The Screen, Norwich Cathedral,* watercolour, *c.*1807. 36 × 27·2cm.

50 Dedication to Sir Henry Englefield, *Miscellaneous Etchings*, 1811. 30·4 × 22·7cm.

51 *The Old College House, Conway, North Wales, Miscellaneous Etchings*, 1811. 30·4 × 21·4cm.

52 *Trees in Duncombe Park, Yorkshire*, pencil study for etching. 20·6 × 13·1cm.

53 *Trees in Duncombe Park, Yorkshire, Miscellaneous Etchings,* 1811. 21·6 × 14·5cm.

54 *South Gate, Yarmouth*, etching, *The Architectural Antiquities of Norfolk*, 1811–18. 25·7 × 34·1cm.

55 *St Benet's Abbey*, etching, *The Architectural Antiquities of Norfolk*, 1811–18. 27·6 × 38cm.

56 *Grand bonfire at the Yarmouth Festival*, soft ground etching with colour, d. 19 April 1814. 19 × 27.6cm.

57 *A Street in Yarmouth*, pencil, *c.*1815. 9·1 × 7·9cm.

58 *Arches of the Cloister of St Georges de Boscherville*, pencil and sepia, d. 3 July 1818. 1821 (possibly because sepia was added at later date). 34·1 × 22·3 cm.

59 *West Front of Rouen Cathedral*, etching, *The Architectural Antiquities of Normandy*, 1822. 54·7 × 39·8cm.

60 *Château Gaillard*, monochrome drawing in preparation for etching, Tate Gallery, insc. 'Sketched July 24, 1818'.

61 *Château Gaillard*, etching, *The Architectural Antiquities of Normandy*, 1822. 25·4 × 35·5cm.

62 *Crypt of the Abbey Church of the Holy Trinity at Caen*, etching, *The Architectural Antiquities of Normandy*, 1822. 25·4 × 35·5cm.

63 *Castle at Dieppe*, etching, *The Architectural Antiquities of Normandy*, 1822. 25 × 42·2cm.

64 *The Town of Mortain with Mont St Michel*, sepia, 1820–23. 28·3 × 46·3cm.

65 *Mont St Michel*, watercolour, c.1825, 30·7 × 52·9cm.

66 *View on the River Sarthe near Alençon*, pencil, d. 24 December 1823. 23·3 × 33·2cm.

67 *Old Houses in Normandy*, watercolour, 1823–28. 46·2 × 34·2cm.

68 Study for a painting of Norwich Castle, black and white chalk on bluish-grey paper, d. 5 April 1825, 21·6 × 32·7cm.

70 J. M. W. Turner, *Norham Castle on the Tweed*, mezzotint, *The Rivers of England*, 1823–27. 17·7 × 26cm (engraved area).

71 Drawing after Turner's *Norham Castle on the Tweed*, pencil, 1824–28. 9·5 × 13·7cm.

72 J. M. W. Turner, *The Junction of the Severn and Wye*, mezzotint, 1811, *Liber Studiorum*. 17·8 × 26·2cm.

73 Study after Turner's *Junction of the Severn and Wye*, pencil, c.1832. 9·5 × 14·9cm.

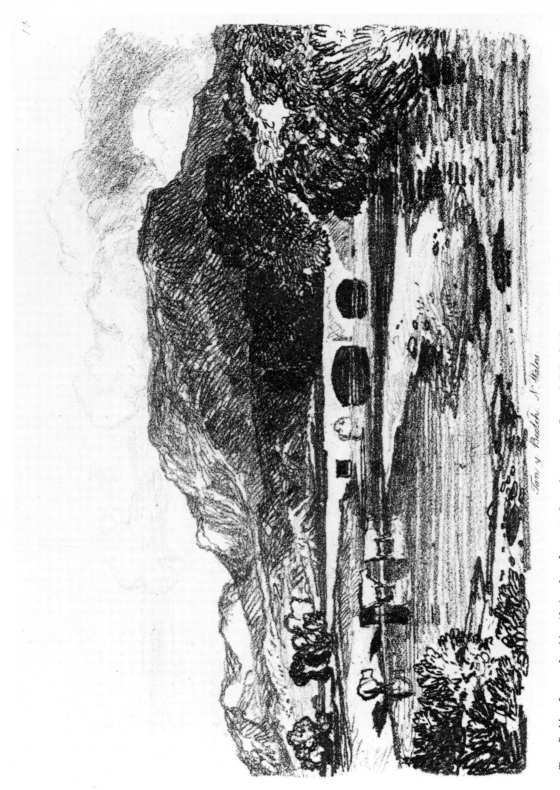

74 *Tan y Bwlch*, soft ground etching (design dates from c.1806). 12·6 × 17·5 cm. Cotman's *Liber Studiorum*, published 1838.

75 *Judgment of Midas*, soft ground etching (design dates from c.1809). 20 × 25·1cm. Cotman's *Liber Studiorum*, published 1838.

76 *Postwick Grove*, black chalk heightened with white, *c*.1814. 21·5 × 30·8cm. Cotman's *Liber Studiorum*, published 1838.

77 *Postwick Grove*, soft ground etching. 15·1 × 22·5cm. Cotman's *Liber Studiorum*, published 1838.

78 *Hayboat on the Medway*, pencil, probably 1828. 15·9 × 22·2 cm.

79 *Dreadnought on the Thames*, pencil, d. 8 January 1828. 9·8 × 16·9cm.

80 *Fire at Vinegar Works on the Yare*, pencil with coloured chalk and touches of body colour, 1829. 23·8 × 33·6cm.

81 *Bamborough Castle*, watercolour, *c*.1830. 24·9 × 39·2cm.

82 *Postwick Grove* (−29), watercolour, *c*.1835. 21 × 29cm.

83 *Cader Idris*, watercolour, *c.*1835. 20·3 × 30cm.

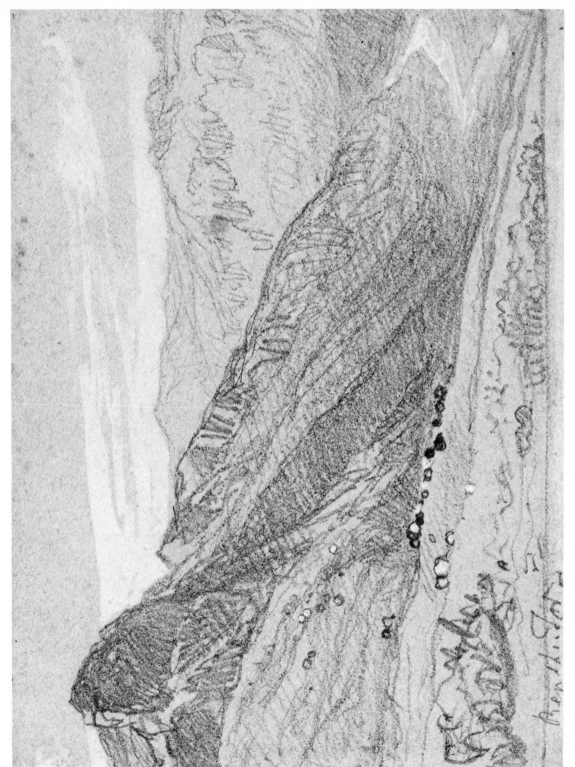

84 *Benthe Tor*, pencil heightened with white on blue paper, c.1836. 18·3 × 24·3cm.

85 *Mountains and Lake, North Wales*, pencil heightened with white on brown paper, *c.*1839. 23·3 × 33·3cm.

86 *Heidelberg Castle*, pencil, c.1834. 22·6 × 33·3cm.

87 *Cephalus and Procris*, black and white chalk on brown paper, *c.*1839. 15·7 × 23·3cm.

88 *Landscape with Boys Fishing*, brush and ink with body colour on blue paper, probably 1839. 27·8 × 37·5 cm.

89 *River Bank with Trees*, black and white chalk on brown paper, d. 2 October 1841. 13·2 × 37·3 cm.

90 *The Wold Afloat*, black and white chalk on grey paper, d. 19 October 1841. 22·2 × 37·3cm.

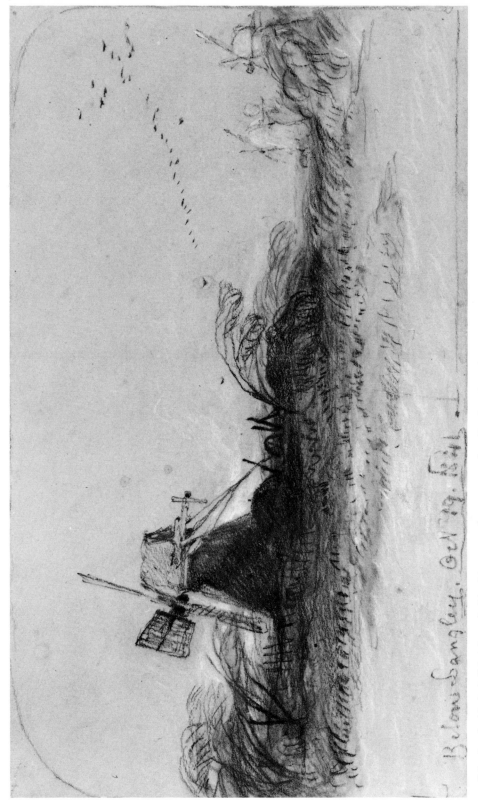

91 *Below Langley*, black chalk heightened with white on grey-brown paper, d. 19 October 1841. 18·7 × 31·7cm.

92 *Sky Effect near Yarmouth*, black chalk heightened with white on blue paper, 1841. 9·9 × 21·5cm.

93 *Storm off Cromer*, black and white chalk on brown paper, d. 14 November 1841. 27·6 × 54·7cm.

94 *Blofield: The Old Yarmouth Road from Norwich*, black and white chalk on brown paper, 1841. 34·9 × 46cm.

95 *Blofield: The Old Yarmouth Road to Norwich*, black and white chalk on grey-brown paper, d. November 1841. 36·8 × 54·1 cm.

96 *Hollow Way at Blofield*, black chalk heightened with white on blue paper, 1841. 23·1 × 33·6cm.

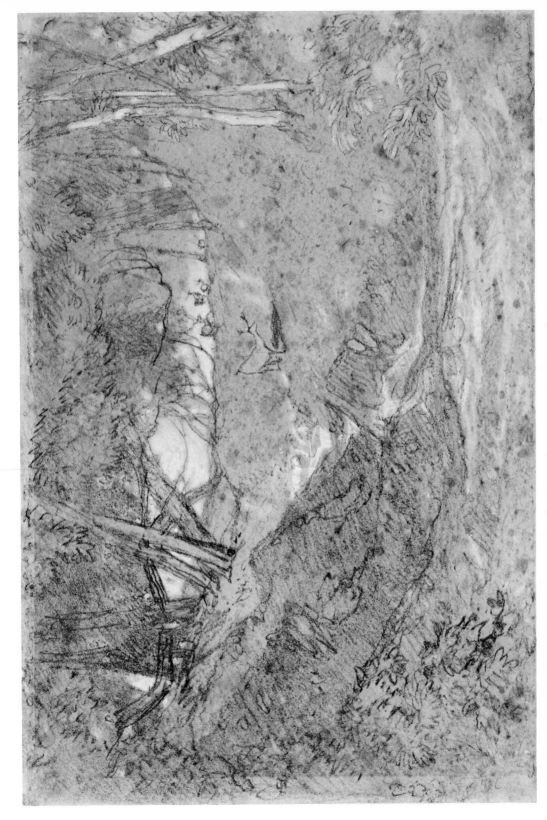

97 *At Blofield near Norwich, Deer in a Glade*, pencil, chalk and body colour on brown paper, 1841. 18·1 × 26·9cm.

98 *The Pound at Blickling*, black and white chalk on grey paper, d. 10 November 1841. 26·4 × 37·1cm.

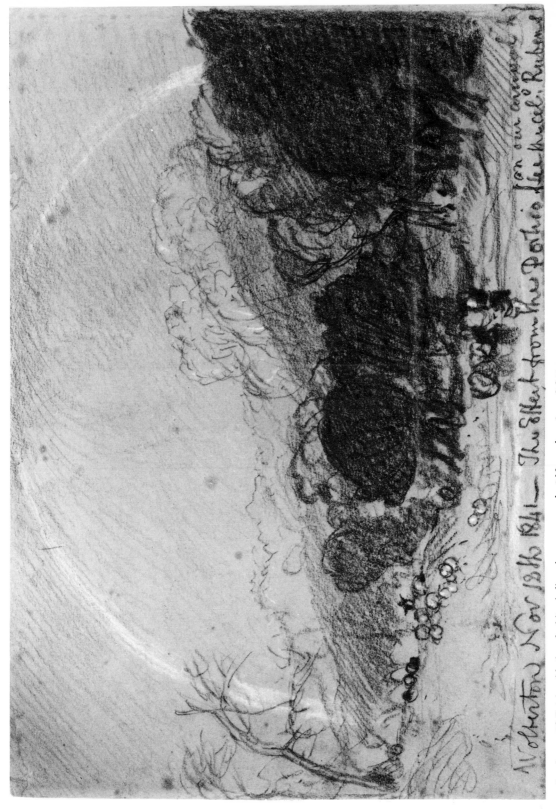

99 *Landscape with Rainbow*, black and white chalk on brown paper, d. 18 November 1841. 18·8 × 27·1 cm.

100 *Mousehold Heath* (–164), black and white chalk on brown paper, 1841. 13·1 × 18·6cm.

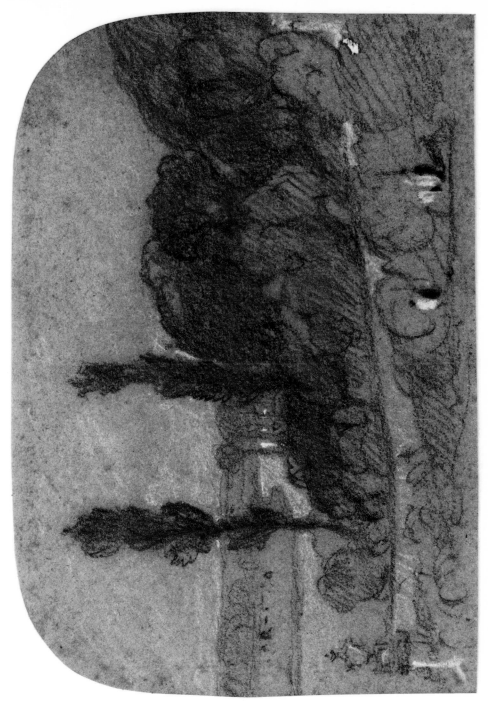

101 *From my Father's House at Thorpe*, black and white chalk, 1841. 12·9 × 18·3 cm.

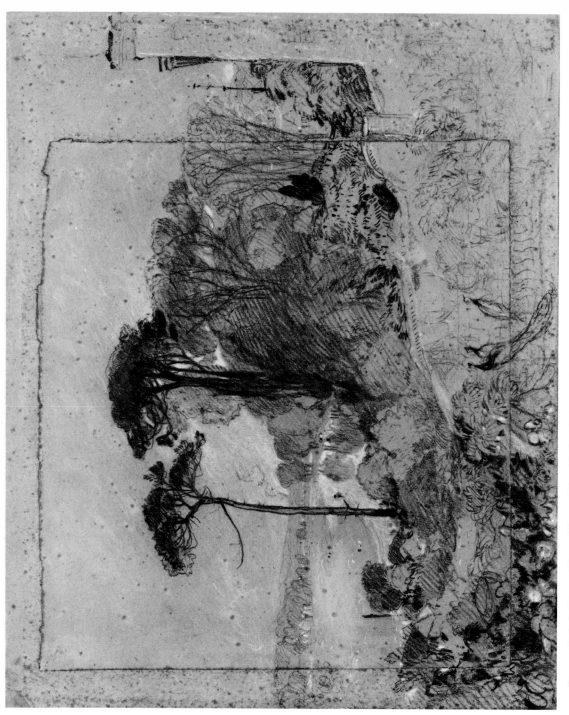

102 *From my Father's House at Thorpe: View with Firs*, black and white chalk on grey-brown paper, 1841. 31·1 × 37·6cm.